Idioms at Work

Ve

Illu

Language Teaching Publications 1987

1

This edition edited by Michael Lewis

Based on **Idioms 1** published in 1980 by
Public Service Commission of Canada
Language Training Branch
English Program Development Unit
Bisson Centre
Ottawa Canada K1A 0M7

The original material was by Vera McLay, edited by Howard B Woods, Michael Sutton and Cornelius von Baeyer.

Many people have contributed to the French, Spanish, German and Italian translations. We are particularly grateful to Norma Fernandez, Angeles Broca, Anne Péchou, Judith Fleming and Christophe Dupin.

Reprinted 1988, 1990, 1992, 1998

ISBN 0 906717 60 4

Printed in England by Commercial Colour Press, London E7.

2

Introduction

What are idioms?

Idioms are phrases where the whole phrase means something different from the meaning of the separate words. If you are *fed up,* you are bored and unhappy, but the whole phrase has nothing to do with *feed;* if something works out alright *in the long run,* it means *in the end, when the whole process is finished,* but it has nothing to do with *running.*

All languages have idioms, but an idiom in one language may have no direct equivalent in another. This means when you learn a new language you have to learn the idioms as complete phrases.

Idioms are very common in spoken English; they are less common in written English, or more formal situations. In English, in particular, idioms are very often used in business contexts to help to create a relaxed atmosphere. Most of the idioms in *Idioms at Work* are common in situations which can occur in commerce, business or government departments. Someone whose English is very good, but who uses no idioms, can sound formal and rather impersonal, and, therefore, a little unfriendly. For this reason, idioms are important in building a pleasant atmosphere, and helping to make sure that your business meetings do not seem 'cold'.

Are idioms always appropriate?

Some idioms are very informal and are only used in conversations among friends. Most of the idioms in this book, however, will sound completely natural in any ordinary discussion or business meeting.

Understanding and using idioms

Sometimes students do not feel comfortable using idioms. They find it difficult to believe that the unusual combinations of words can be used with the special meaning of the idiom. Anyone who wants to use English, however, must be ready to *understand* idioms if they are used by other speakers. Very often, native speakers of English do not even know that they are using these special expressions. They do not think they are "difficult", so do not know that a foreign listener may have trouble with them.

How to use *Idioms at Work*

Idioms at Work can be used with a teacher, or you can use it alone, for self-study.

You can work through the book Unit by Unit, or you can pick and choose those units which you think will particularly help you.

After each set of five Units there is a Test. You can use this in two ways:

— before you work through the Units, to see if you already know any of the expressions
— after you have studied the Units, to check that you have learnt the expressions and to see how much you have improved.

Probably the best way to use each unit is as follows:

1. Look at the list of expressions at the top of the chapter. Try to say the phrases out loud a few times. Don't worry if they sound a little strange at first.

2. Work through the material in the book, situation by situation, filling in the appropriate expression.

3. Try to say the phrase which contains the idiom a few times out loud so that it feels natural to you.

4. A few days later go through the material again, or check the Test to make sure that you have learnt the expressions.

For each situation we have given French, Spanish, German and Italian equivalents — sometimes idiomatic, sometimes translations or paraphrases. In addition, after each situation there is a non-idiomatic English equivalent. These, of course, are only to help you understand exactly how the idiom is used.

If you are using *Idioms at Work* in class, in addition to working through the material in the book, you may like to practise the idioms by writing your own situational dialogues, or by using the idioms in mini-roleplay situations.

However you use *Idioms at Work*, we hope you will enjoy reading the material, and that it will help make your English more friendly and more natural.

Contents

The French, Spanish, Italian and German given in this book was prepared in each case by more than one native speaker of the language. The suggestions which are made are intended only to be a help in understanding the language in the particular context in which it occurs in this book. It is not suggested that the foreign language equivalents are *exact* equivalents of the English idioms.

A TOSS UP

1. Time Expressions

a. at the eleventh hour

b. every now and then

c. it's high time

d. once in a blue moon

e. in the nick of time

f. in no time

g. in the long run

h. on the double

i. for the time being

j. out of the blue

OUT OF THE BLUE

WOW!

Fill in the blanks with the best idiom from the list above. Use the equivalents below each situation to help you. Answers at the back of the book.

1. I hear you've given up sailing.

    Not completely. I still go _every now & then_ ,
    but I'm much more interested in windsurfing nowadays. It's more
    of a challenge, but I still go out in a boat occasionally.

    from time to time; sometimes b

    de temps en temps   *de vez en cuando*

    ab und zu   *di tanto in tanto*

2. Hi, Pete. I see you're still driving that old wreck. I thought you were going to buy a new car.

No, I've changed my mind. But I'm getting rid of my car. I'm going to use taxis in future.

Really — that'll be much more expensive.

No, _____ I think it'll actually be cheaper.

How do you work that out?

in the end; in the final result

à la longue   *a la larga*

auf lange Sicht   *alla lunga*

3. I hear you had a pretty rough weekend.

Yes we had a bit of a fire at home.

What happened?

We went shopping and left a heater on. It short-circuited and started a fire. We arrived _____ _____ to call the fire brigade before it was a real disaster.

That must have been terrible!

at the last possible second

juste à temps   *justo a tiempo*

gerade noch rechtzeitig   *giusto in tempo*

4. Michael, the boss wants to see you in his office right away.

O.K. I'll be there in a couple of minutes. I just want to finish this letter.

You'd better forget the letter and get in there _____ _____. You know he hates to be kept waiting.

fast; quickly

au plus vite; sur-le-champ   *en seguida; inmediatamente*

schnellstens; aber mit Tempo! *immediatemente*

5. What beautiful flowers!

Thank you. My husband sent them for our anniversary.

Lucky you. I love flowers but I have to buy them for myself. I'm lucky if I get them _____ _____ from my husband. He can't even remember the date of our anniversary.

Well, nobody's perfect.

very rarely &

très rarement;	*muy de vez en cuando;*
tous les 36 du mois	*cada año bisiesto*
einmal in hundert Jahren;	*ogni morte di papa*
einmal alle Jubeljahre	

6. I wish Jack was here.

Why?

This tape recorder is making a funny noise and I need it now. The last time this happened Jack fixed it _____ _____.

Let me have a look at it. I may not be as fast as Jack but I can probably fix it.

Thanks, that's very kind of you.

in a very short time   &
*(used with verbs of **doing** something)*

en un rien de temps;	*en un minuto; al instante*
en un tournemain	
ruckzuck	*in un minuto*

7. It looked as if there was no chance of an agreement.

Why not?

Well the management said they had to move by the end of June and the Union said definitely 'No' and threatened to strike.

What happened?

Well it looked impossible but _____
_____ somebody said why not the 7th of July and everyone agreed, and that was that.

at the last possible moment

à la dernière seconde   *en el último instante*

in letzter Minute; fünf vor zwölf   *all'ultimo momento*

8. Hey, Sue. I've just heard our department's moving to the new building. Is it true?

It seems to be. The boss announced it at our section meeting this morning. I hope we move soon. I'm sick of these so-called temporary buildings.

_____ we moved. This place is falling apart.

it's long overdue (that)

il est grand temps   *ya es tiempo; ya es hora*

es ist höchste Zeit   *e'ora*

9. Did you hear that Brian is leaving his wife?

Who told you that?

He did. We were having coffee this morning and _____
_____ he announced that he and his wife are breaking up. He didn't say much but I gather there's a third person involved.

suddenly, without warning; unexpectedly

tout à coup   *de repente*

aus heiterem Himmel   *tutto d'un tratto*

10. Mr Stuart in room 411 is asking if he can go home tomorrow, doctor. Not yet I'm afraid, nurse. I'd rather keep him here _____ _____ We need to do a few more tests.

temporarily; at the moment

pour le moment   *por el momento*

bis auf weiteres   *per il momento*

2. Being Confused

a. slipped my mind
b. I've lost my train of thought
c. can't make head nor tail of
d. on the tip of my tongue
e. caught between two stools
f. It beats me.
g. I haven't a clue
h. racking my brains
i. are over my head
j. couldn't get a word in edgeways

Fill in the blanks with the best idiom from the list above. Use the equivalents below each situation to help you. Answers at the back of the book.

1. (Mary and Alice are talking)
    Mary   What we really need is a new approach to work. I was thinking abo...

    Jack   Hi Mary. Did you have a nice weekend?

    Mary   Not bad! And yourself?

    Jack   Can't complain. Can't complain.

    Alice   What were you going to say?

    Mary   I can't remember. With Jack interrupting me, _____
    _____.

    I forgot the idea I was talking about b
    j'ai perdu le fil   *perdí el hilo*
    ich habe den Faden verloren   *ho perdo il filo*

2. Tom, What's the capital of Yugoslavia?

Don't ask me. _____. You know I'm hopeless at geography.

I have absolutely no idea ♂

je n'ai pas la moindre idée   *no tengo la menor idea*

ich habe keine Ahnung   *non ho la più pallida idea*

3. Have you worked out how to assemble that bookcase yet?

No, I've looked at these instructions for the last hour but I _____ them. And the diagrams don't help — they're even more confusing.

Let me have a look. Two heads are better than one.

I can't understand them ⌒

je n'y comprends rien   *no puedo descifrarlo*

sie sind mir schleierhaft   *non riesco a decifrarle*

4. Well, did the boss say yes? Two extra staff?

Are you kidding? The minute I hinted at extra staff he started talking about budget restrictions, cutbacks, over-spending in other sections — he went on and on for at least an hour. I tried to interrupt a couple of times but I _____.
After a while I just gave up and left.

had no chance to say anything

je n'ai pas pu placer un mot　　　　*no pude decir ni palabra*

ich bin überhaupt nicht zu Wort　　*non ho potuto metter bocca*
gekommen

5. Right off we go. Are you ready?

Yes, but we're a bit early aren't we. The show doesn't start till half past seven.

Yes, but don't forget we promised to pick Claire and Jack up. Their car's being fixed.

Oh yes, sorry. It completely _____ _____
_____ _____. It's a good job you reminded me!

escaped my memory; I forgot (it)

ça m'est sorti de l'esprit　　　　*se me pasó por completo; se me olvidó*

es ist mir total entfallen　　　　*mi è passato completamente di mente*

14

6. If I book a ticket today I save £80 on the fare; but then I'll have to spend two extra days in Paris doing nothing.

Unless Pierre can see you on Friday instead of Monday.

Yes, but I won't know that until tomorrow afternoon, and by then it's too late to book the cheap air ticket.

It sounds as if you're _____.
I'd book now if I were you and take a chance — after all, two free days in Paris wouldn't be too awful!

finding it difficult to choose between two alternatives e

le cul entre deux chaises   *en una encrucijada*

(du sitzt) zwischen zwei Stühlen   *non sai che pesce pigliare*

7. Quick Terry. What's the name of the chap who gave the first talk this morning?

Oh, let me see. It's an unusual name — Polish I think. Kowalski? No it's not that, but it is something like that. That's annoying. It's _____ but I just can't think of it.

Oh-oh! He's coming over here, and I want to ask him to give a talk at our next training session. It looks bad if I can't even remember his name.

*something I can **almost** remember*   a

je l'ai sur le bout de la langue   *lo tengo en la punta de la lengua*

es liegt mir auf der Zunge   *ce l'ho sulla punta della lingua*

8. How come the new photocopier isn't working?

Don't know. _____. The repairman just left fifteen minutes ago and said it was working fine.

I know how to make it work. How about plugging it in!

I can't understand it   f

je ne comprends pas   *ni idea*

das ist mir ein Rästel   *non lo capisco*

9. How's your computer course going?

I'm not really sure, to tell you the truth.

What do you mean, you're not sure?

Well, I understand the manuals — at least I think I do — but I don't understand half of what the prof talks about. He uses too many technical words. I'm afraid his lectures _____
_____.

Maybe I should have taken the introductory course.

are too difficult for me

sont trop difficiles pour moi;　　　*son demasiado difíciles para mí*
me dépassent

sind eine Stufe zu hoch für mich　　*sono troppo difficili per me*

I'VE LOST MY TRAIN OF THOUGHT!

10. What are you scratching your head for?

I've been _____
all morning trying to remember the name of the company that gave that course in Transactional Analysis. I know they're based in Bristol and the name's on the tip of my tongue but I just can't remember it.

Why don't you look it up in the files?

Because I can't remember what I filed it under.

I've been thinking hard

je me creuse la cervelle　　　　　*devanando los sesos; quebrando la cabeza*

ich zerbreche mir den Kopf　　　*mi sto spremendo le meningi*

3. Knowing or Agreeing

a. on the same wavelength

b. know the ropes

c. put your finger on it

d. straight from the horse's mouth

e. put two and two together

f. rings a bell

g. see eye to eye

h. heard it on the grapevine

i. took the words right out of my mouth

j. knows it like the back of his hand

Fill in the blanks with the best idiom from the list above. Use the equivalents below each situation to help you. Answers at the back of the book.

1. (Two close friends.)
    How's married life treating you?

    Pretty good.

    Now that the honeymoon's over are you still getting on all right together?

    Fine, we sometimes disagree on small things but we usually _____ on anything important.

agree
voyons les choses du même oeil   *estamos de acuerdo*
wir sind einer Meinung   *siamo d'accordo*

2. Hey, Jill. Does the name Alan Garside mean anything to you?

Alan Garside. Let me see . . . um . . . That name _____ _____ but I still can't place it.

There's a message on my desk asking me to call him but I haven't a clue who he is.

sounds familiar ƒ

me dit quelque chose   *me suena; me resulta familiar*

kommt mir bekannt vor   *mi suona familiare*

3. How are you getting along with your new supervisor?

Great, really terrific. He's got some really modern ideas about how to organize the work. He's introduced flexible hours and has promised us a really effective career development programme. He's doing all the things I always said we should be doing.

Sounds like you two are _____.

Right, I think we're really going to enjoy working together.

having the same sort of ideas α

sur la même longueur d'onde   *en la misma onda*

(liegen) auf dergleichen Wellenlänge   *sulla stessa lunghezza d'onda*

4. Did you buy a map?

No but don't worry. I used to live round here so I _____ _____.

know the place extremely well
le connaît comme le fond de sa poche   *lo conozco como la palma de su mano*
kenne es wie meine Westentasche   *lo conosce come il palmo della sua mano*

5. Hey, have you heard the latest? Old Smith is leaving.

That's too good to be true. Who told you?

I _____ . Everyone seems to be talking about it.

You know you shouldn't believe all those rumours.

Come on! There's usually some truth in them. They say he's got a better job.

I'll believe it when I see it.

heard a rumour
c'est un bruit qui court   *lo he oido por ahi;*
                             he oldo rumores

es ist mir zu Ohren gekommen;   *me lo ha detto un uccellino*
(ich habe etwas läuten gehört)

8th's bugging Me.

6. What's bugging Bill? He hasn't been himself lately.

I'm not sure but I think he's still mad about not getting that promotion last month.

I think you've _____. Just the other day I heard him complaining that good employees aren't appreciated around here.

given exactly the right answer C

tu as visé juste	*has dado en el clavo*
die Sache auf den Punkt gebracht	*ho messo il dito nella piaga*

7. Have you heard there's going to be a big reorganisation?

There's always rumours about a reorganisation.

This isn't just a rumour. I got it _____
_____.

You mean the Personnel Director himself?

That's right.

Well, I guess he should know.

from the authoritative source d

de très bonne source	*le sé de buena tinta*
aus sicherer Quelle; *aus berufenem Mund*	*l'ho saputo da fonte sicura*

8. So you're getting the boss's job, eh!

No I'm not. Who told you that?

Nobody *told* me. But, when I see a guy measuring the boss's office and moving the furniture around the way you've been doing, I can _____.

Look, please don't say anything. The official announcement won't be made until next week.

Oh, I won't breathe a word. You can count on me.

make a deduction from the evidence ℮

c'est aussi sûr que deux et deux font quatre

zwei und zwei zusammenzählen

llegar a la conclusión; sacar una conclusión

arrivare alla conclusione

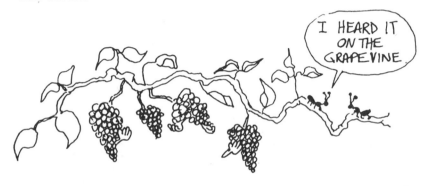

I HEARD IT ON THE GRAPEVINE

9. Well, Brian, you must excuse me. I'm due at a meeting. But Bob here will show you around some more and introduce you to the rest of the staff.

Thank you very much for spending so much time with me, Mr Hudson.

I'm leaving you in good hands. Bob has been with us for 15 years and, believe me, he _____.
You couldn't have a better guide.

knows all aspects of the job; ᵇᵒ
has a lot of knowledge or experience of the subject

connaît les ficelles

kennt die Spielregeln

conoce su trabajo

se ne intende

10. Doug, have you seen item four on the agenda for tomorrow's meeting?

You mean the proposal on a computerized information system?

Right. That's the one.

Yeah. I've read it and I think we need to do a very careful cost analysis before we do anything.

That's just what I was going to say. You _____ _____.

Since we obviously see eye to eye on it, let's hope other people do too.

said exactly what I was going to say   ぴ ぃ

tu m'as sorti les mots de la bouche   *me quitaste la palabra de la boca*

du hast mir das Wort aus dem Mund genommen   *mi ha tolto la parola dalla bocca*

WE MUST BE ON THE SAME WAVELENGTH

4. Failure

a. was a flop

b. missed the boat

c. bite off more than (you) can chew

d. caught red-handed

e. got out of hand

f. on the blink

g. haven't got a leg to stand on

h. go to pieces

i. draw a blank

j. get (your) act together

Fill in the blanks with the best idiom from the list above. Use the equivalents below each situation to help you. Answers at the back of the book.

1. When is Jerry expected back at work?

Not for a long time. I went to see him at the weekend and he was in a very poor way.

Still, eh? I knew that when his wife died he just _____ _____ .

Yes, since then he's had one nervous breakdown after another.

Poor chap. Let's hope they can do something to help him.

was completely unable to function as an ordinary person

il s'est écroulé   *quedó deshecho*

er hat durchgedreht   *si è lasciato andare*

2. Hi, Ron. How did your talk go?

Horrible! I tried to explain our new approach to T-groups but it was over their heads. Most of them left before I finished. The whole thing _____.

It couldn't have been as bad as all that. I just got a request from someone who was there, who wants you to give your talk at another conference.

Forget it!

was a total failure

a été un fiasco   *fue un fracaso*

war ein Reinfall   *fu un fiasco completo*

3. I tell you, Andy, I'm going to take that guy to court.

What on earth for?

For wrecking my car.

Come on, Bill! You were too close. It's the driver behind who is responsible, not the one in front. If you take him to court, you _____. The law says it was you who was in the wrong.

haven't got a valid claim

tu n'as pas d'argument valable;   *no tienes suficiente argumento*
tu n'as pas le moindre chance

du hast nichts vorzuweisen;   *non ha argomenti validi*
du hast keine Chance

4. (A couple returning to an estate agent)

Good morning. Still house-hunting?

Yes, but not very successfully. I guess we really _____ _____ when we didn't take that bungalow last week.

That was certainly a bargain.

You wouldn't have another one like that, eh?

There's one very similar in Mount Avenue but it's £3,000 more.

missed our chance

on a râté l'occasion   *perdomos la oportunidad*

wir haben die Gelegenheit verpaßt   *abbiamo perso un' occasione*

YOU HAVEN'T GOT A LEG TO STAND ON!

5. Linda, would you give Rick a hand with the report on our staffing requirements for next year?

I offered to help him but he insisted he could handle it on his own.

Well, the Management Committee wants the report by Monday and Rick says he'll need help to have it ready on time.

So now he admits he _____. I told him so.

tried to do more than he could manage
avait les yeux plus gros que le ventre   *el que mucho abarca poco aprieta*
er hat sich übernommen   *ha fatto il passo più lungo della gamba*

6. Did you find that book I asked you to get me?

No. I'm afraid not. I tried the departmental library and town library but (I) _____.
Then I rang three different bookshops but none of them had ever heard of it.

Maybe I gave you the wrong title. Let me check.

Now you tell me!

didn't get the desired results; didn't have any success

ça n'a rien donné   *no encontré nada*
ça n'a pas marché

aber Fehlanzeige!   *ho fatto un buco nell'acqua*
ich hatte kein Glück

7. Robert and Jill are on holiday next week.

I know. And I've promised that that work for Harpers will be ready by next Thursday; and we'll have to get all the details we need from the agents. And I've promised to spend Tuesday at the Trade Fair.

If we don't _____ we are going to be in trouble next week. It sounds as if we've bitten off more than we can chew.

organise this well

si on ne s'organise pas   *organizamos las cosas bien*

(sich) zusammenreißen   *se non ci organizziamo*

8. (A special news bulletin)

The police were called in last night during a demonstration in Parliament Square. What started as a peaceful march, to protest at the present high level of unemployment, soon _____ _____ when demonstrators started throwing stones and exchanging blows with the police. Ten people, including three policemen, were injured.

became uncontrollable and disorderly

la police a été débordée   *se armó la pelotera*

ist außer Kontrolle geraten   *e' diventato incontrollabile*

9. Hey, did you hear that Saunders has been fired?

No kidding! What happened?

He was robbing the company.

Is there any chance they made a mistake? He seemed to be such an honest person.

There's no mistake. The night guard caught him in the director's office, with the safe open, stuffing money into his briefcase. He was _____.

What a surprise! It's difficult to believe.

caught in the act

pris en flagrant délit;   *lo pillaron con las manos en la masa*
pris, la main dans le sac

auf frischer Tat ertappt   *colto con le mani nel sacco*

10. Oh, no!

What's the problem?

The photocopier has broken down again.

Better send for the repairman.

Not again! That's the third time this week this machine's been _____.

out of order; broken down

est en panne   *se ha estropeado*

ihren Geist aufgegeben hat   *si è rotta*

HE BIT OFF MORE THAN HE COULD CHEW.

5. Success or Strong Interest

a. kill two birds with one stone

b. made quite a name for him/herself

c. snowballed

d. over the moon

e. turn (someone) on

f. keep an eye on things

g. in the bag

h. on the ball

i. call the tune

j. went like a bomb

(**Note** in American usage *to bomb* is to *fail*; in British English *to go like a bomb* means *success*)

Fill in the blanks with the best idiom from the list above. Use the equivalents below each situation to help you. Answers at the back of the book.

1. I sometimes wonder who's running this country nowadays.

    What do you mean?

    Well, from what I see in the papers and on TV, it's the unions and big business that are _____ these days.

    directing everything; in charge

    mènent la barque

    estan a cargo
    lleven las riendas; dirigen

    die erste Geige spielen die;
    die sagen wo es lang geht

    hanno le redini in mano

2. You look pleased.

I am. That big deal with the Germans — they've agreed so I'm
_____. It was very important
for my career that they agreed.

Congratulations. No wonder you're pleased!

extremely pleased

enchanté, ravi   *muy contento*

überglücklich   *al settimo cielo*

3. Do you think this new line will sell in Italy?

Well, a lot depends on the agent — look what happened last year
in France, but Mirelli are _____
_____, they know what they're doing.

So you're fairly confident about Italy.

understand the situation well
dans le coup   *al corriente*
auf Zack (sien)   *in gamba*

KILLING TWO BIRDS

4. How did the meeting go?

It _____. Everyone had something to say. It was very lively.

was very successful

était passionant

war ein Bombenerfolg

tuvo mucho éxito

è andato splendidamente

5. Have a good trip to Spain?

You must be joking. It was terrible.

Why? What went wrong?

Well, we all thought the contract for next year was _____ _____, just a few details to settle, but no. Suddenly they announce they are considering new suppliers; our price is too high; they want to change the technical specification. Everything was wrong!

Goodness — did you get it all sorted out?

a certainty

dans le sac

schon in der Tasche haben

resuelto

in tasca

WITH ONE STONE

31

6. (A guest speaker is introduced)

Until a few years ago there was little talk in Canada of the need for gun control. Outbreaks of violence in the recent past, however, raised the question of the need for stricter gun control and, in many parts of the country, small groups of concerned citizens got together to try to solicit support in their campaign to force the government to pass strict legislation against the carrying of firearms. The movement has _____ in recent months and a national committee has now been formed. With us tonight we have the chairperson of that committee, Henrietta Perkins. Good Evening, Ms Perkins . . .

increased a lot quickly

a fait boule de neige　　　　　　　*tomado fuerza*

ist lawinenartig angewachsen　　*si è esteso a macchia d'olio*

7. Who's the new Assistant Deputy Manager going to be, do you know?

Yes, it was announced this morning. It's Jennie Pinkerton.

That name rings a bell.

It should. She _____ in her last department. She only joined the company as a middle manager 18 months ago and now she's a senior executive.

Wow. That's fast. She really must have what it takes.

got a reputation

s'est fait un nom;　　　　　　　*se ha hecho famosa*
s'est fait une réputation

hat sich einen Ruf erworben;　　*si è fatto un nome*
hat sich einen Namen gemacht

8. Where are you going, Fred?

Don't worry. I won't be long. I'm just going down to the Post Office.

Oh, do you think you could _____ and post this registered letter for me please.

Sure.

32

do two things at the same time

faire d'une pierre deux coups

zwei Fliegen mit einer Klappe erschlagen

matar 2 pájaros de un tiro; matar 2 pájaros de una pedrada

prendere due piccioni con una fava

9. That new chap in the accounts Department is very strange, isn't he?

Nigel? Oh he's all right. He doesn't say much.

He never spoke all day. Just sat at the keyboard pulling funny faces.

That's Nigel. People leave him cold but computers really
_____. Give him a computer and he's happy.

excite, stimulate (someone)

il a ça dans la peau

(auf Computer) fährt er voll ab

le estimulan

lo stimolano

10. Who's looking after the budget while you're away?

Jack's doing the day-to-day work but I've asked Peter — he's the Finance Director — to _____.
I don't think there'll be any problems. Jack's very sensible.

take an interest in; supervise

ouvrir l'oeil　　　　　　　　　　　*supervisa*

die Sache im Auge zu behalten　　*tenere le cose sott' occhio*

YOU'VE REALLY MADE QUITE A NAME FOR YOURSELF

TEST 1 (Chapters 1~5)

This is a test of some of the idioms in the first 5 Chapters. An English equivalent is given for each item.

The exact number of words required is indicated each time by the number of blanks.

Use this test to check what you know either before or after you have studied Chapters 1-5. The answers are on page 95.

1. How come this cassette won't play when I switch it on?

   It _____ _____. I don't know anything about cassette players.

   I don't understand it

2. You've been reading the newspaper for the last two hours, Robertson. It's _____ _____ you started doing some work.

   long overdue (that)

3. Do the letters P.P.B.S. mean anything to you?

   Yes. That _____ _____ _____. I think they stand for Programme Planning and Budgeting Systems.

   stirs a memory

4. Do you like the Rolling Stones' music?

   I'll say. Any kind of rock music really _____ _____ _____.

   excites me

5. How was Howard's presentation of the new long range planning proposal?

   It _____ _____ _____ _____. Everyone thought it was great. It was very well received.

   was a great success

6. We'll have to put some controls on this flexible hours business. Everyone's arriving late and leaving early. It's a real mess.

I agree. Things are _____ _____ _____ _____.

going out of control

7. Would you give me a hand with the annual report, please?

I offered to help you but you said you could do it on your own.

Don't rub it in. I admit I _____ _____ _____ _____ _____

_____ _____.

took on more than I can manage

8. Could you run off 10 copies of each of these documents for me, please?

I'm sorry. The machine's _____ _____ _____.

out of order; broken down

9. Since you're going to pick up Nancy from school why don't you

_____ _____ _____ _____ _____ _____ and drop me at the swimming pool on your way there.

do two things at the same time

10. Did you explain your new idea to the boss over lunch?

No way. He talked so much I _____ _____ _____ _____ _____ _____.

didn't have a chance to say anything

11. How was the party last night?

It _____ _____ _____. Only six people showed up.

They expected 40 people, so at least there must have been plenty to eat and drink.

was a total failure

12. Did you remember to bring the book you promised me?

I'm sorry. It completely _____ _____ _____. I'll bring it tomorrow.

escaped my memory

13. Do you and your wife go to the cinema much?

Only _____ _____ _____ _____ _____. I think the last film we saw was 'Last Tango in Paris' when it first came out.

very rarely

14. I realize that, in the short term, switching to a computerized system seems very expensive. However, _____ _____ _____ _____ it will save us millions.

over a long period

I HAVEN'T GOT A CLUE...

15. Who told you Janet's getting the Director's job?

I heard it _____ _____ _____. I don't remember exactly who said it.

in informal office talk

16. It's true about school finishing early today!

Who told you?

I got it _____ _____ _____ _____ _____.

You mean the Headmaster?

That's right.

from the highest authority concerned

17. I've been studying the instructions for assembling your new model airplane, son, and I _____ _____ _____ _____ _____ _____ them.

It's easy, Daddy. I'll show you.

don't understand at all

18. I advise you not to take this complaint any further, Jack. You _____ _____ _____ _____ _____ _____ _____.
The supervisor was within his rights.

don't have a valid argument

19. We only expected about 6% this year, so everyone is _____ _____ _____ with 8%.

very pleased

20. If you want someone who really _____ _____ _____, ask Shirley. She's been to Turkey several times. She'll be able to tell you anything you want to know.

has a lot of experience

6. Money Matters

a. in the red
b. sell like hot cakes
c. square up
d. What a rip-off!
e. flat broke
f. over the odds
g. corner the market
h. cut corners
i. can't make ends meet
j. cost you an arm and a leg

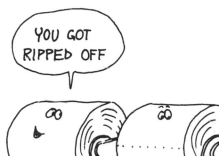

Fill in the blanks with the best idiom from the list above. Use the equivalents below each situation to help you. Answers at the back of the book.

1. (In a restaurant)

   Don't worry, I'll pay.

   No, no. I think you paid last time I was here. It's my turn.

   No, it's OK, I'll get it.

   No, I'd rather you let me pay this time.

   It's too late now. The waiter's taken it.

   Well I insist we _____ later. I want to pay my fair share.

   settle, balance account
   (usually between private people not businesses)

   on réglera ça plus tard   *haremos las cuentas*

   abrechnen   *dividiamo le spese*

2. Got your tickets for the Liverpool game yet?

Not yet. There's still plenty of time.

Are you kidding? You'd better buy them today or you'll miss the boat. Those tickets always _____.

Come on. I know there's always a big demand for them but the game's months away.

sell quickly

partent comme des petits pains   *se vende como pan caliente*

verkaufen sich wie warme Semmeln   *vanno a ruba*

3. What sort of discount did they ask for?

35% — it's a bit _____ but I think it's probably worth it. I think they'll provide better service than any other distributor in the area.

I suppose we'll have to agree to it, then.

above the average, more than normal

plus que d'usage   *superior a lo normal*

uber dem Durchschnitt;   *più del solito*
gesalzen

4. Excuse me, I think there must be a mistake on the bill. What's this 15% at the bottom?

That's the service charge, sir.

What do you mean, service charge? The service was terrible . We had to wait 20 minutes before we even got the menus. The food was cold. The steak was tough and overcooked. The chips were soggy. And now you want to charge an extra 15%. _____

It's an excessive charge

c'est du vol   *es un robo; es una estafa*

so ein Nepp!   *che ladri!*

5. Did you go house-hunting at the weekend again?

Mmm, but I'm beginning to give up hope of ever finding a good house at the right price.

Did you see the development I was telling you about?

Yes. We went there on Sunday. I like the layout but the construction is not very good. You can tell they've _____ _____ to keep the costs down.

done things badly to save money

rogner sur le marchandise;   *economizado*
faire des economies de bouts de
chandelle

an allen Ecken gespart   *economizzare*

6. I see World Business Machines has just bought out two more of their competitors. They are obviously out to _____ _____ in office machines.

Yes, they'll soon have the complete monopoly. It's high time the government did something about these giant corporations.

establish a monopoly

(s') accaparer le marché   *acaparar el mercado*

den Markt zu erobern   *accaparrarsi il mercato*

7. Say, Bob. Could you lend me a fiver until tomorrow?

Sorry, Gerry. I'm afraid I'm _____.
In fact, if I didn't have a season ticket I wouldn't be able to get home tonight.

without any money
fauché; sans le sou   *sin un duro*
pleite; vollkommen blank   *al verde*

WE CAN'T MAKE ENDS MEET...

8. So, to sum up, gentlemen, there simply isn't enough demand for our product. We've been operating _____
_____ for the last year, and the only way to get into the black is to lay off some of the workers.

at a loss
être à découvert   *a fondo perdido*
in den roten Zahlen   *in perdita, in passivo*

42

9. Hello, I didn't know you worked in a bar. When did you leave your office job?

I haven't left. I'm still doing the same job.

So this is a bit extra?

Not really extra, I couldn't support my family and keep up the mortgage payments on my other salary.

I know what you mean. We _____ these days, either. Do they need another barman here?

can't live comfortably on the money you earn

je n'arrive pas à joindre les   *no nos llega para vivir tampoco*
deux bouts

wir kommen mit dem Geld nicht aus   *non sbarchiamo il lunario*

10. Where are you taking your wife to celebrate your wedding anniversary?

We're going to Luigi's.

Don't go there. It's far too expensive. It'll _____
_____.

I suppose so but their food is excellent.

Listen. I know a new French restaurant where the food's just as good, if not better, for about half the price.

Oh really. Where is it?

cost you more than it is worth
ça te coutera les yeux de la tête   *costará un ojo de la cara*
das kostet eine schöne Stange geld!   *costerà un occhio della testa*

7. Extreme or Excess

a. the last straw
b. I've had enough
c. that takes the biscuit
d. we're splitting hairs
e. the tail wagging the dog
f. get carried away
g. to add insult to injury
h. laying it on thick
i. pretty far-fetched
j. making a mountain out of a molehill

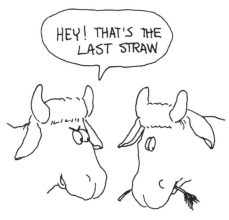

Fill in the blanks with the best idiom from the list above. Use the equivalents below each situation to help you. Answers at the back of the book.

1. That damn technician completely ruined my presentation.

   Oh no! What happened?

   He told me he'd checked all the equipment. I switched on the tape recorder, but it's only got one speed — the wrong speed. Then I went to the flip chart; the minute I touched it, one of the legs broke.

   Oh no! That presentation was really important for us.

   I didn't give up. I smiled at everybody and switched on the projector; the clown had put the film on backwards. That was (1) _____ _____. I couldn't take any more. I gave them a coffee break so I could fix things up.

   I hate to say 'I told you so' but I did say you were (2) _____ _____ with all that equipment.

   I know! I guess you were right.

(1) the final problem in a series of problems

(2) carrying something to extreme or excess

(1) ça a été la goutte d'eau (qui a fait   *(1) el colmo*
    déborder le vase)

(2) tu exagérais   *(2) exagerando*

(1) das war de Gipfel   *(1) il colmo*

(2) ziemlich dick auftragen;   *(2) esageravi*
    übertreiben

THE TAIL
WAGGING
THE DOG

2. Look here, everyone, this discussion seems to be getting out of hand. As I see it we are all agreed on the general principles, and what we're now discussing are minor details. I think _____ _____ and as a result, wasting time. Let's stick to important matters.

arguing about small, unimportant differences

on coupe les cheveux en quatre   *buscarle siete pies*

wir treiben Haarspalterei   *si sta spaccando il capello in quattro*

3. It's a crisis — an absolute crisis.

Come on now, Mike. The situation isn't that serious. It's a relatively minor problem, and we can deal with it before it gets out of hand.

It's a crisis, I tell you.

Look, I think you're getting things all out of proportion. You're _____. Maybe we should leave it, and see how we feel tomorrow.

thinking a small problem is a big one

tu en fais une montagne   *estás haciendo una montaña de un*
                                     grano de arena

du machst aus einer Mücke einen   *fare di un granello una montagna*
Elefanten

LAYING IT
ON THICK

4. What are you looking so mad about?

It's Mike again. Every time there's a little problem he gets it all out of proportion.

I know what you mean.

I'm sick of him running into my office and telling me we've got a crisis on our hands. I tell you _____
_____. If he tries to tell me there's a crisis on one more time, I'll throw something at him.

I have come to the end of my patience

j'en ai par dessus la tête

mir reicht's

ya me colmó la paciencia;
no lo aguanto más
ne ho abbastanza

5. I'm fed up with our so-called service units telling us operations managers how we should be doing things.

'So-called' services is right. They're supposed to give us the back-up services we ask them for. Instead, they keep telling us to change our system to suit them.

Things are completely turned around. It's a case of _____
_____ .

the normal situation is reversed

c'est la monde à l'envers

es ist eine verkehrte Welt

darle la vuelta al asunto

il mondo alla rovescia

6. What are you shaking your head about?

I've just finished reading Steve's list of ways of motivating employees. I really don't think many of his ideas are reasonable or practical. Most of them are _____.

rather exaggerated; out of touch with reality

être tiré par les cheveux   *un poco exageradas*

ziemlich weit hergeholt;   *un po'troppo esagerato*
an den Haaren herbeigezogen

7. Say, Steve, about that list of suggestions you gave me on ways of motivating employees . . .

What did you think of it?

Well, I really liked one or two of your ideas, but I'm afraid I found some of them rather extreme.

Perhaps I _____ with some of them. I've probably been reading too much psychology recently.

exaggerated, was too positive

je me suis laissé emporter

habe ich mich mitreißen lassen

me he dejado llevar

mi sono lasciato transportare

8. The Electricity Board really are the limit.

What have they done now?

Well, you know the electricity was off most of yesterday and we've had three or four blackouts in the last three months and now, (1) _____ we never got the normal bill, but this morning we got a threat to cut us off if we didn't pay within seven days!

That's incredible; (2) _____ .
You should send them a bill for all the frozen food you've had to throw out.

(1) to make things worse

(2) that's the limit

(1) le comble

(1) para colmo

(2) il ne manquait plus que ça

(2) eso fue lo último

(1) das Ganze noch schlimmer zu machen

(1) otre al danno la beffa

(2) das schlägt dem Faß den Boden aus

(2) questo è il massimo

48

8. Compromise or Balance

a. take what he says with a pinch of salt

b. meet them halfway

c. give him a break

d. make allowances for

e. sit on the fence

f. a happy medium

g. let sleeping dogs lie

h. bend over backwards

i. the best of both worlds

j. sleep on it

Fill in the blanks with the best idiom from the list above. Use the equivalents below each situation to help you. Answers at the back of the book.

1. The Bonus Account gives maximum growth of capital, while the High Income Account is best if you want a regular income. If you need a bit of both, I think you'll find the High Yield Account is _____.

a compromise

un juste milieu

ein goldener Mittelweg

llegar a un acuerdo; encontrar el justo medio

un giusto compromesso

2. That guy in the stockroom is so slow it's unbelievable. I just spent half an hour waiting for him to find me a box of notepads.

Come on, Phil. You have to _____ the fact he's only been here a week and it's a pretty complicated stock system.

judge the situation by the circumstances

tenir compte du fait que   *tener en cuenta*

gewisse Zugeständnisse machen   *tener conto del fatto che*

3. (Three months later)

So help me, I'm going to do something about that stock clerk. He's been here for months now, but he hasn't improved at all. I've warned him enough. I've had enough. He'll have to go.

Oh, come on, Phil. _____. He deserves another chance. He's trying.

offer him another chance

donne-lui une chance   *dale otra oportunidad*

gib ihm eine Chance!   *dagli un po'di respiro*
laß ihn in Ruhe!

A HAPPY MEDIUM

4. But you don't know my parents. They've got such old-fashioned ideas. They want me to be home by 11o'clock on Saturday nights.

That seems a bit strict but, you know, if you want them to give you more freedom, you've got to be willing to _____ _____ sometimes. You can't expect to get your own way in everything.

give up part of what you want to reach agreement

couper la poire en deux   *tienes que dar tu brazo a torcer*

dich mit ihnen auf dem halben Weg   *venirgli incontro*
treffen

5. Was Anderson serious when he said the company's going to lay off a couple of hundred men?

Oh, he's always spreading rumours. There's usually something in what he says but you should always _____ _____.

assume only part of what he says is true

il faut en prendre et en laisser   *creerle la mitad de lo que dice*

es nicht immer für bare Münze   *credere alla metà di quello che dice*
nehmen

6. How do you like having old McKay for a boss?

Look. He may be old and slow but he looks after his staff. He'll _____ to help any of us.

Good for him. It's pretty rare to find a boss who'll do all he possibly can for his staff. Usually all they care about is their next promotion.

make a great effort

se met en quatre   *hace todo lo posible; se mata*

er reißt sich ein Bein aus   *farsi in quattro*

7. Donaldson really bugs me. When there's a problem around here he never supports one side or the other. He always tries to keep everyone happy, so he never ends on the wrong side.

Right. I've noticed he always _____ no matter what's being discussed.

It's high time he learned that the only thing that does is make him unpopular with us all.

does not want to choose or decide

ne veut pas se mouiller   *nunca se decide*

setzt sich zwischen alle Stühle   *tenere il piede in due staffe*

8. I'm really flattered to be offered promotion, but I'm not sure how I feel about moving to the North of Scotland.

I realize it's a big decision to make, Bert. I don't expect you to give me an answer immediately. Why don't you go home and _____. Talk to your wife and we can discuss it again tomorrow. I'll need your decision by the end of the week.

think about it for a while

la nuit porte conseil   *lo piensas bien;*
                              lo consultas con tu almohada

überschlafen Sie die Sache   *dormirci sopra*

9. Is Sally in?

I hope you're not going to bother her again with this business about Gordon.

I'm still not happy about it.

Why don't you _____?
Bothering her about that again isn't going to change anything. The decision was final.

I still want to put my point of view. I'm convinced it was the wrong decision.

Well, I'd drop the matter if I were you.

avoid making more trouble on the same issue

pourquoi remuer le passé   *lo dejas tal cual*

warum willst du schlafende Hunde   *perchè stuzzicare il cane che dorme?*
wecken?

10. With the Bonus Account you get 1% extra interest, but you have to give a month's notice if you want your money, with the Ordinary Account you can have your money immediately but you only get the normal interest. With the new Golden Account you get

_____ .

all the advantages

vous n'avez que des avantages   *todas las ventajas*

haben Sie nur Vorteile   *i vantaggi di entrambi*

BENDING OVER
BACKWARDS

9. Complaining or Commiserating

a. **pull the wool over other people's eyes**

b. **a stab in the back**

c. **pay lip service to**

d. **fed up to the teeth with**

e. **get away with murder**

f. **That's below the belt.**

g. **talk behind (his) back**

h. **take (someone) for granted**

i. **fob (someone) off**

j. **isn't pulling (his) weight**

Fill in the blanks with the best idiom from the list above. Use the equivalents below each situation to help you. Answers at the back of the book.

1. I know what I'd do to those kids next door if they were mine.

   I agree. They're completely out of hand.

   It's high time their parents did something. They let them _____
   _____ .

   Young parents are all the same these days. Anything goes as far as they're concerned.

   do bad things without being punished
   s'en tirer impunément
   sie erlauben ihnen alles
   salirse con la suya
   lasciare fare totto quello che vogliono

HITTING BELOW THE BELT

2. I'm (1) _____ Linda Brown; the boss thinks she's a great worker because, whenever he's around, she really tries to impress him. But when he's not there she doesn't do any work at all.

I hate people like that who try to (2) _____ _____, but I suppose one of these days he's going to find out the truth.

(1) annoyed by someone's behaviour over a long period of time

(2) deceive someone into thinking well of them

(1) par dessus le tête	*(1) hasta las narices*
(2) jettent de la poudre aux yeux de quelqu'un	*(2) engañar a alguien*
(1) ich habe die Nase gestrichen voll mit	*(1) averne fin sopra i capelli*
(2) einem Sand in die Augen streuen	*(2) gettare fumo negli occhi*

3. You seem to have upset Roger. He says you promised to pick him up at the station and then you forgot all about it.

I'm afraid so — I was busy, it just slipped my mind.

He's pretty annoyed. He says it's not the first time you've forgotten.

Oh come on! _____. There was a misunderstanding about three years ago. I don't think he should mention that again after such a long time.

that goes against one's sense of justice and sportsmanship

c'est un coup bas   *es un golpe bajo; no hay derecho*

das ist unter der Gürtellinie   *questo è un colpo basso*

4. How are things going on the selection board, Sue?

Don't talk to me about that board. I've had enough of them.

Why?

Well, they talk about equal opportunities a lot, but when it comes to making a decision on a candidate, it's a different story. They bring in all kinds of things that have nothing to do with your ability to do the job.

I agree with you. It's not enough to _____ a principle. You've got to do something about it.

show support by words but not by actions

lancer des paroles en l'air   *lanzar palabras al viento*

Lippenbekenntnis (für ein Prinzip)   *condividere a parole*
abzugeben

5. It's about time somebody told Jack that every member of a team has to do his share of the work.

Mmm, I've noticed he (1) _____.

Of course, it's our own fault. We should tell him to his face that he isn't doing his fair share.

You're right. Instead of telling him to his face, all we've done is (2) _____.

(1) doesn't do his fair share of the work

(2) discuss him when he isn't there

(1) il ne fait pas sa part
(2) parler derrière son dos

(1) no cumple con la parte que le
corresponde; no hace lo que le toca

(2) hablar a sus espaldas

(1) er sienen Beitrag nicht leistet
(2) hinter seinem Rücken geredet

(1) no fa la sua parte
(2) parlare alle spalle

6. I've just spent half an hour trying to get an answer to a very simple question from the Town Hall.

I bet the first person told you to call another number, and then they told you somebody was out, then they gave you some vague answer that didn't mean anything.

Exactly, they must think the public are stupid. They couldn't _____. I insisted on being given the proper facts, but it was hard work and took a long time.

satisfy me with unsatisfactory information

me renvoyer comme un malpropre   *malinformarme*

mich nicht mit leeren   *scaricarmi*
Versprechungen apspeisen

7. Gosh, I really miss Rachel. This new secretary doesn't seem to know what's going on half the time.

Mm, I've noticed.

I'm really sorry now I didn't tell Rachel what a good job she was doing.

Well, we all _____. Maybe she wouldn't have left if we'd told her how much we appreciated her.

took the benefit of her good work without commenting on it

on considerait ça comme acquis   *no hemos apreciado su trabajo*

haben sie als Selbstverständlichkeit   *non apprezzare il suo lavoro*
angenommen (od. betrachtet)

8. How's Colin feeling about what happened last night?

Pretty bad, I'm afraid, and I don't blame him. At least thirty people promised to vote for him but didn't in the end. And they were people he trusted completely.

Yeah. When they voted for Peter it was _____ for Colin.

That's politics, I guess.

an act that hurt a friend or a trusting person

un coup de couteau dans le dos   *una puñalada por la espalda;*
                                          una mala jugada

ein Dolchstoß   *una pugnalata alla schiena;*
                                          un tiro mancino

10. Meeting People

a. feeling a bit under the weather

b. have a night out on the town

c. talking shop

d. Thanks all the same.

e. I don't feel up to

f. put (my) foot in it

g. to put (someone) out

h. It's a small world, isn't it.

i. to bump into (someone)

j. Talk of the devil!

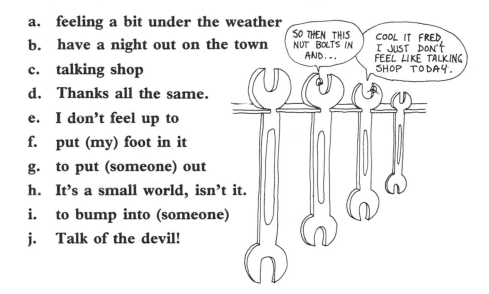

Fill in the blanks with the best idiom from the list above. Use the equivalents below each situation to help you. Answers at the back of the book.

1. Good night, Dick. It was a great party. Thanks for the invitation.

   I hope you aren't leaving already. It's still early.

   I think I'd better get home to bed. I'm _____ _____. I had a touch of the flu last week, and I've had a very busy week. I hope you don't mind.

   Oh no, of course not. I hope you're soon all right again.

   Don't worry. I'm sure an early night will cure me.

   slightly ill

   je ne suis pas en forme;   *no me siento bien*
   je ne me se sents pas bien

   ich fühle mich etwas angeschlagen   *non mi sento in forma*

2. Mike *(to Ann)* ... and as for Andy, he spends a lot of time hanging about the typing pool talking to the girls . . .

Ann   Girls! You've said the magic word, Mike.
(Andy arrives)

Mike   Oh, hi Andy. _____.
I was just telling Ann, here, about you.

Andy   Nice things, I hope.

Mike   Of course, what else?

(Expression used when the person you have just been talking about arrives.)

Quand on parle du loup on   *hablando del rey de Roma*
en voit la queue

wenn man vom Teufel spricht!   *parli del diavolo e spuntano le corna*

3. (A few minutes later)

What are you looking so guilty about?

You know me and my big mouth. I just _____
_____ again.

Who did you insult this time?

Well, I was talking to that tall girl over there, Ann, and telling her about the people at the office and . . . uh . . . well nobody told me she was Andy's fiancée . . .

Aw Mike! I can't take you *any*where!

made a social mistake

j'ai mis les pieds dans le plat;   *metí la pata*
j'ai fait une gaffe

ins Fettnäpfchen getreten   *ho fatto una gaffe*

FEELING UNDER THE WEATHER

4. Get out your dress. We're going to _____.

What are we celebrating?

I've just been offered that job in Bristol.

Great! Now that's worth celebrating. Give me ten minutes and I'll be ready to go.

go out to celebrate

on va faire le fête   *celebrar*

ausgehen um zu feiern;   *darsi alla pazza gioia*
einen draufmachen

5. Where are you going to, John?

The Central Station.

Jump in. We'll give you a ride. It's on our way home.

That's OK. My wife's picking me up in a couple of minutes.

_____ .

(Polite expression used when you completely refuse an invitation or offer.)

merci quand même   *gracias de todos modos*

trotzdem vielen Dank   *grazie lo stesso*

6. Come on, come on. This is a party, not the office. You've been sitting here talking about work for the last hour. Come on and join the party.

OK. We're coming.

But you have to promise you'll stop _____.

speaking about your work

parler du boulot   *de hablar del trabajo*

über die Arbeit reden   *parlare del lavoro*

GEE... TALK OF THE DEVIL...

7. Excuse me. The restaurant seems to be full. Do you mind if we share this table?

No. Have a seat . . . For heaven's sake! Pete Fraser! Fancy meeting you so far from home.

Frank Harris! I thought you'd be slaving away back at the hospital.

Me to! I didn't know you were planning a holiday. Imagine us (1) _____ each other in Rome of all places.

(2) _____.

(1) *meeting by accident*

(2) *(Expression used when you meet someone you know whom you did not expect to see there.)*

(1) *tomber sur*
(2) *que le monde est petit*

(1) *me encontre con*
(2) *qué pequeño es el mundo; el mundo es un pañuelo*

(1) *wir uns hier über den Weg laufen würden*
(2) *die Welt ist doch klein*

(1) *incontraci per caso*
(2) *come è piccolo il mondo*

8. Do you fancy going to the concert at the City Hall tonight?

Oh, John (1) _____ getting the car out again. I've had a really rough day at the office. I'm very tired.

Well, shall I come round and pick you up? It's on my way, anyway.

Are you sure? I don't want (2) _____.

No, that's fine. I'm sure you'll enjoy the concert when you get there. It'll help you to relax.

(1) *I don't have the strength to*

(2) *inconvenience you*

(1) *je ne suis pas en forme; je ne me sens pas de taille*

(2) *te déranger*

(1) *ich habe keine Lust; ich bin nicht dazu fähig*

(2) *ich will dir keine Umstände machen*

(1) *no tiene ganas de*

(2) *molestarte*

(1) *non me la sento di*

(2) *non voglio scomodarti*

TEST 2 (Chapters 6~10)

This is a test of some of the idioms in chapters 6-10. An English equivalent is given for each item.
The exact number of words required is indicated each time by the number of blanks.
Use this test to check what you know either before or after you have studied Chapters 6-10.
The answers are on page 96.

1. I've got to find a job that pays more than the one I've got now. We're up to our ears in debt and we _____ _____ _____ _____.

   can't earn what it costs to live

2. It isn't a crisis at all. It's only a minor problem. You're _____ _____ _____ _____ _____ _____ _____.

   thinking a small problem is a big one

3. Don't believe everything Shirley tells you. You should _____ what she says _____ _____ _____ _____ _____.

   not believe all she says

4. I typed that report five times because Mr. Robertson kept making changes to it. But then, when he asked me to do it again with double spacing instead of single spacing that _____ _____ _____ _____. I told him he could type it himself.

   the final problem in a series of problems

5. We agreed to have a night out on the town to enjoy ourselves not to talk about work. Let's stop _____ _____ .

discussing work

6. It's high time someone told Gordon that each member of a team has to do a fair share of work.

Mm, I've noticed he isn't _____ _____ _____ on our team.

doing his share of work

7. You'd better hurry up and buy your tickets for the annual dinner. They're _____ _____ _____ _____.

selling quickly

8. It's not enough to _____ _____ _____ _____ a principle. You have to prove you believe it by your actions.

show support by words only and not by actions

ALRIGHT YOU GUYS! QUIT TRYING TO PULL THE WOOL OVER MY EYES AND GET BACK TO WORK!

9. You mean to say he charged you twenty pounds for a five pound ticket. _____ _____ _____!

   that's robbery

10. I'm (1) _____ _____ _____ _____ _____ _____ Muriel. She never gives a definite opinion one way or the other. She always (2) _____ _____ _____ _____.

    (1) annoyed by
    (2) does not want to choose or decide

11. Claude will do everything possible for his staff. He'll _____ _____ _____ to help any one of them.

    make a great effort

12. What a surprise (1) _____ _____ our next door neighbours while we were camping in France this summer.

    Yes. (2) _____ _____ _____ _____ _____ _____?

    (1) meeting by accident
    (2) (Expression used when you meet friends where you did not expect to see them.)

13. That chap John Richards is really deceitful. He doesn't do any work but he's fooled the boss into thinking he's a great worker.

    I can't stand people like that who _____ _____ _____ _____ _____ _____ _____.

    deceive others into thinking well of them

14. This house is really badly constructed. The builder obviously tried to _____ _____ to keep his costs down.

    do something in the cheapest way

66

15. I don't think it's worth arguing about. It's not very important.
I think we're _____ _____.

arguing about small, unimportant details

16. Me and my big mouth. I really _____ _____ _____ _____
_____ today. I was telling somebody in the office how badly the
boss treated his secretary and when I turned around, there he was,
standing in the doorway.

made a social mistake

17. You two obviously don't see eye to eye but surely you can find
_____ _____ _____ that you can agree on.

a compromise

18. They tried to _____ _____ _____ with "I'm afraid he's out
of the office", but I insisted on getting some hard facts.

satisfy me with an unsatisfactory answer

11. Giving or Seeking Information

a. read between the lines

b. keep me posted

c. off the top of my head

d. ask point blank

e. speak off the cuff

f. give me a rundown

g. off the record

h. spilled the beans

i. drop you a line

j. don't beat about the bush

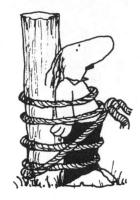

KEEPING HIM POSTED

Fill in the blanks with the best idiom from the list above. Use the equivalents below each situation to help you. Answers at the back of the book.

1. Bad news, Stephen. Our after-dinner speaker just called to say he can't come because the airport's closed. You'll have to fill in for him.

   Please find somebody else. You know I'm no good at making speeches even when I have time to prepare them. I'm even worse when I have to _____.

   give a talk without preparation

   improviser   *improvisar*

   aus dem Handgelenk sprechen   *improvvisare*

68

2. Say, Bob, what was the Director's answer when you asked him if the rumours were true?

He was pretty vague, I'm afraid.

Maybe your question wasn't direct enough.

It couldn't have been more direct. I _____
_____ if there would be any redundancies in the next few months.

asked directly

j'ai demandé carrément;
j'ai demandé à brûle-pourpoint

ich habe rundheraus gefragt

le pregunté directament

ho chiesto chiaro e tondo

3. (A week later)

OK Bob. We know you were called up to the Directors' meeting this morning. What did they say about redundancies?

Well . . . uh . . . you see . . . it seems that for the time being, at least and . . . if the marketing report confirms the estimated trend and provided . . .

Come on, Bob. Get to the point. _____.
We want a straight answer to the question. Are there going to be redundancies or not?

don't avoid the question

ne tournez pas autour du pot

schleich nicht wie eine Katze um
den heißen Brei

no te vayas por las ramas

non perdiamoci in chiaccahere;
non menare il can per l'aia

4. Things seem to be going quite well in our Caribbean offices. Did you read their latest reports?

Yes, I did. On the surface, things seem to be going well but if you _____ I think you'll find there are some problems.

guess what is left unsaid

lisez entre les lignes　　　　　　*lees entre líneas*

zwischen den Zeilen lesen　　　　*leggete fra le righe*

5. Good luck on this trip to the Far East.

Thanks, Frank. I'll have a full report for you when I get back next month.

I know we'll have a complete report in a month but I'd like to get some feedback before then, so _____, eh?

Don't worry. I'll ring you and let you know how things are going.

make sure I am informed

tiens-moi au courant　　　　　　*manténme al día;*
　　　　　　　　　　　　　　　　manténme al corriente

halten Sie mich auf dem laufenden　*tienimi al corrente*

6. We're really going to miss you two, after all these years having you as neighbours. Now you're going to be five hundred miles away in the north of Scotland.

Don't worry. As soon as we're settled, I'll _____ _____ and let you know how things are going.

write you a letter

je vous écrirai un mot   *te escribiré*

werde ich was von mir hören lassen   *ti scriverò due righe*

OFF THE CUFF

7. That seems to take care of the business on the agenda. But before you leave I'd like each of you to (1) _____ _____ on your major projects. Let's start with you, Shirley. How long will it take before the new computerized system completely replaces the manual one?

I'm afraid I didn't bring the reports with me and I don't remember the exact dates for the completion of the various phases . . .

I just want a guesstimate.

Well, (2) _____, I'd say the new system will be in place within three months. I'll check the details and let you know this afternoon.

(1) give me a summary

(2) from memory

(1) me donner un aperçu   *(1) me hagais un resumen*

(2) de mémoire   *(2) por lo que puedo recordar*

(1) mir einen Überblick geben   *(1) darmi un resoconto*

(2) aus dem Stegreif gesprochen   *(2) da quello che mi ricordo*

8. Hey, you promised you wouldn't tell the boss we took Friday afternoon off.

Don't blame me. I didn't tell him. It was Ernie who _____ _____.

But he was with us!

He must have felt guilty and decided to confess.

admitted something

a vendu la mèche   *se le escapó*

nicht dichtgehalten hat   *ha vuotato il sacco*

9. Come on, John. We're old friends. I promise I won't print it unless it's announced officially.

OK, but it's strictly _____. If any of it gets into the newspapers before the Minister announces it officially, I'll be in serious trouble.

confidential; not to be published

confidentiel   *confidencial*

ganz im Vertrauen   *confideziale*

STOP BEATING ABOUT THE BUSH!

12. Things Going Wrong

a. **stumbling block**

b. **to start from scratch**

c. **throw a spanner in the works**

d. **can't get the hang of it**

e. **in a rut**

f. **going round in circles**

g. **caught on the wrong foot**

h. **upside down**

i. **is in for**

j. **scraping the bottom of the barrel**

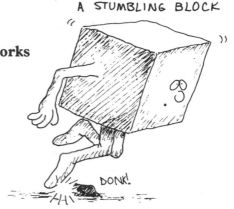

A STUMBLING BLOCK

Fill in the blanks with the best idiom from the list above. Use the equivalents below each situation to help you. Answers at the back of the book.

1. Are you busy at the moment?

   Busy? We're snowed under. Overtime every day. We were really _____ by that order from Spain. It arrived the same week that the holiday season started.

   unprepared

   pris de court　　　　　　　　　*desprovistos*

   auf dem falschen Bein erwischt　　*ci è arrivato tra capo e collo*

2. What made you decide to apply for that job in Belgium?

Well you know, I've been working for the same company for ten years now. I like my work but I feel I'm _____ _____. The job just isn't as interesting or challenging as it used to be.

In that case a change will probably do you good.

in a dull routine

ça devient routinier   *se está haciendo una rutina*

im gleichen Trott (sein)   *mi sto fossilizzando*

3. Am I glad to see you!

What's the matter?

It's this new film projector. I've been trying to thread a film for the last twenty minutes but I just _____ _____. I could put a film on the old projector in no time, but this one's got me beaten.

Let me have a try.

don't know how to make it work

je n'ai pas le tour de main   *no sé como hacerlo funcionar;*
                                          no le encuentro la maña

komme nicht auf den Dreh   *non so da come farlo funzionare*

SCRAPING THE BOTTOM
OF THE BARREL...

4. How are the negotiations for the new pay deal going?

They've broken down completely. The union side walked out yesterday.

That's a surprise. The last I heard everything was going well.

The Union (1) _____. They suddenly demanded a four-day week. We can't agree to that. That's (2) _____.

(1) caused a difficulty

(2) the problem point

(1) a mis des bâtons dans les roues

(2) le hic

(1) wurf uns einen Knüppel zweischen die Beine

(2) das steht der Sache im Weg; eine Hürde

(1) provocó un problema

(2) el punto problemático

(1) mettere il bastone fra le ruote

(2) lo scoglio; ostacolo

JOE'S IN A RUT.

5. What's in the crate?

I don't know. I can't get it open.

I'm not surprised. It's _____. You're trying to open the bottom. Turn it over. It's easier to open from the top.

the wrong way up

sens dessus dessous

steht auf dem Kopf

de cabeza; al revés

sottosopra

6. When's Phil due back from his holiday?

Not for another couple of weeks. Why do you ask?

I'm afraid he _____ an unpleasant surprise. They've reorganized his section out of existence.

is unable to avoid; will certainly get

va certainement avoir;   *se va a encoutrar*
peut s'attendre à

ihm steht (eine böse Überraschung)   *va incontro a*
bevor

I CAN'T SEEM TO GET THE HANG OF IT!

7. Any ideas on what to do about sales in France? They are not going well this year.

More newspaper ads? Bigger discount to the dealers?

Oh come on, that's _____. We need some new ideas, something really different.

using ideas which are only just of acceptable quality

c'est ringard   *haciendo uso del último recurso*
c'est pas genial

das ist wirklich das Letzte vom   *questo è toccare il fondo*
Letzten

8 Look, it's been a long day and we're all tired. I don't think we're going to solve all these problems today.

Wait a minute. I think we came up with some pretty good ideas.

That was a couple of hours ago. Since then we've been repeating the same things. We're _____ _____. Let's leave it till tomorrow. Our minds will be clearer in the morning.

talking without any progress

on tourne en rond   *dándole vueltas al asunto*

wir bewegen uns nur im Kreise   *ci stiamo affannando senza risultati*

9. I've tried to re-arrange the desks to find space for two more people, but they won't all fit.

Why have you left Peter's office as it is now?

Well we can't change everything!

With this sort of problem it's best _____ _____. It usually saves time in the end.

to begin from nothing

recommencer à zéro   *volver a comenzar desde el principio*

ganz von vorne anzufangen   *ricominciare do zero*

13. Contradicting or Disagreeing

a. beside the point

b. barking up the wrong tree

c. I've got a bone to pick with you.

d. So what?

e. doesn't hold water

f. take exception to

g. Come off it!

h. is at odds with

i. putting the cart before the horse

j. that's all very well and good but

Fill in the blanks with the best idiom from the list above. Use the equivalents below each situation to help you. Answers at the back of the book.

1. Hold on a minute. There's no point discussing how we're going to give the course before we establish the course objectives.

   You're right. We're _____. Let's set the objectives first and then we can discuss how to achieve them.

   getting things in the wrong order
   on met la charrue devant les boeufs   *haciendo las cosas al revés*
   zäumen das Pferd vom Schwanz auf   *mettere il carro davanti ai buoi*

78

2. Hello Roger. How are things?

Sally Langton — my favourite personnel officer. Just the person I wanted to see. I _____.

Oh-oh! What have I done now?

You promised to find me a temporary typist two days ago and I'm still waiting.

have something to reproach you about

j'ai un petit compte à régler avec toi   *tengo una cuenta pendiente contigo*

ich habe ein Hühnchen mit dir zu rupfen   *ho un conto da regolare con te*

3. . . . so, in the light of the two points I've just made, I'm sure you'll agree that the decision needs to be looked at again.

(1) _____, Max! You're getting carried away with your own rhetoric. I'm not convinced, whether Dick agrees or not is (2) _____. It's totally irrelevant. And as for your second point, the theory you're basing it on is full of holes — that argument simply (3) _____.

Wait a minute, Anne, I (4) _____ that remark — the theory is fully set out in *Psychology Tomorrow*. Perhaps you should read it!

(1) don't talk nonsense; stop being silly

(2) is not on the subject

(3) is faulty

(4) disagree with, and am annoyed by

(1) arrête de dire des bêtises   *(1) deja de decir tonterías*

(2) sans rapport avec le sujet   *(2) no tiene nada que ver*

(3) ne tient pas debout   *(3) no tiene base*

(4) je ne suis pas d'accord avec   *(4) no admito*

(1) nun mach mal halblang!   *(1) ma dai, non essere stupido*

(2) hat nichts damit zu tun   *(2) non ha niente a che vedere*

(3) ist nicht hieb- und stichfest   *(3) non sta in piedi*

(4) ich nehme (die Bemerkung) übel   *(4) non ammetto*

4. If you guys think that presenting your petition to the board will get action you're _____.

What makes you say that?

Because it's the union that make all the decisions in this area.

choosing the wrong course of action

vous vous trompez royalement　　　*estais enquivocados*
vous vous mettez le doigt dans l'oeil　　*estais en un error*

ihr seid auf dem Holzweg　　　*state bussando alla porta sbagliata*

5. Tell me, Mrs. Stevens, what made you decide to withdraw your child from his previous school and bring him here?

Well, basically because I find that their whole approach _____ _____ my own views on how children should be brought up.

is in conflict with

ne concorde pas avec

geht gegen; widersprechen

no concuerda con;
está en desacuerdo con

contrasta con

6. Doug, the chairman wants the financial reports for the first quarter.

Well, he can't have them until we find out which set of figures is correct. We're working on it night and day and I'd say that we'll have the problem sorted out within a couple of weeks.

_____ it won't satisfy the chairman. He wants those figures today.

Then he can have both sets.

that's fine but

tout çela est b(i)en beau mais

das ist ja alles schön und gut, aber

todo eso está muy bien, pero;
está muy bien, sin embargo

va tutto bene ma

7. Hey, did you hear the news? They've announced a cabinet re-shuffle. Our department has a new Minister.

_____.

Why should I care? At our level it doesn't make any difference who the Minister is.

What an attitude!

(Impolite reply showing that the speaker is not impressed by what has been said.)

et alors?

na, und?

y qué

e allora?

14. The Bureaucracy

a. **Don't rock the boat.**

b. **up in the air**

c. **cut through the red tape**

d. **pass the buck**

e. **pulled a few strings**

f. **blew the whistle on**

g. **snowed under**

h. **get the chop**

i. **go over someone's head**

j. **keep (your) ear to the ground**

THEN HE WENT OVER MY HEAD!

Fill in the blanks with the best idiom from the list above. Use the equivalents below each situation to help you. Answers at the back of the book.

1. I'm going to ask for a transfer to another section.

What's the problem?

It's the supervisor, Bert White. I'm fed up with the way he always tries to _____ when the boss finds something wrong with the section's work.

place the blame or responsibility on someone else

donner tort aux autres　　　　　*echarle la culpa a otro*

dem Schwarzen Peter wegzuschieben　　*fare a scarica barile*

2. Surely you can do without overtime?

Not really. We've got a pile of other rush jobs to do so we're absolutely _____ with work.

Come off it! You people in Accounts don't know what the word means. Now if you were in Personnel . . .

overloaded

débordés (de travail)   *cargados de*

überlastet   *sommersi*

3. It's high time somebody _____ the crew in the mail room.

They're always nipping out for something or other. There's never a full staff there.

Well, I'm not going to be the one who reports them. It's not my job.

reported their behaviour to someone in authority

moucharder   *informe sobre el comportamiento*

(sie) verraten; bloßstellen   *mettere termine al loro comportamento*

83

4. Hello, Debbie. How come you're still here? I thought you were going off to head a new section.

I was supposed to be, but the new organization hasn't been approved yet. It was submitted to the Management Committee but some of the directors have apparently raised some objections. So the whole re-organization is _____ _____ again.

uncertain; undecided

incertain; en suspens   *en el air; indecisa*

hängt noch in der Luft   *per aria*

5. I've had enough with those people in the Accounts Department.

Why don't you deal with the Financial Advisor, Susan Taylor? I find her very helpful.

Well, I don't. She's the one I have the most trouble with. So help me, if I have any more hassle from her I'm going to (1) ____ _____ and take my questions to the Director of Finance.

I wouldn't do that if I were you. You know you just cause more trouble if you don't go through the proper channels.

There you go again! (2) _____.

I'm sick of people telling me not to upset the system. When the system is this bad it should be upset.

(1) go to a higher authority than the person in question

(2) don't cause trouble

(1) passer par dessus   *(1) apelar*

(2) ne poussez pas grand-mère dans les orties   *(2) no busques problemas*

(1) setzte mich über ihren Kopf hinweg   *(1) scavalcare qualcuno*

(2) mach keinen Aufstand!   *(2) non agitare le acque*

6. Believe it or not, I have something good to say about the bureaucracy for once.

Wonders will never cease. What happened?

Remember I told you I needed to get a new passport? Well, I forgot to apply for it until the day before my flight.

Oh no! What did you do?

Well, I took my papers and went to the passport office and explained it all to the lady at the counter. She was very sympathetic and took me to one of the higher-ups and, to cut a long story short, he managed to _____
and get me a new passport in a matter of hours instead of the usual two weeks.

shorten official procedures

simplifier les formalités   *acortar los trámites*

den Verwaltungsweg abzukürzen   *passare per la via più breve*

7. How come Barry's still around. Wasn't he fired? I thought you told me he'd (1) _____.

He did but one of the directors (2) _____ _____ and got him reinstated.

Hmmm. So Barry's got friends in high places, eh? I'd better be careful what I say to him from now on.

(1) been fired

(2) used influence

(1) a été remercié	*(1) lo despidieron*
(2) a tiré les ficelles	*(2) usó su influencia*
(1) ist gefeuert worden	*(1) e'stato licenziato*
(2) hat Beziehungen spielen lassen	*(2) ha adoperato la sua influenza*

8. Have you any idea when Joe returns?

No, nobody has said a word yet.

Well, will you _____ and if you hear anything, let me know as early as possible.

No doubt I'll hear on the grapevine as soon as he is back.

pay careful attention to office talk, rumours etc.

rester aux aguets	*pegar la oreja*
halten Sie die ohren offen	*tenere l'orecchio teso*

15. Winning or Losing

a. is in the running
b. get the better of (someone)
c. get off on the wrong foot
d. in the bag
e. take a back seat
f. to pull it off
g. doesn't stand a chance
h. out on a limb
i. win hands down
j. it's a toss-up

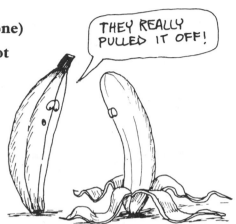

Fill in the blanks with the best idiom from the list above. Use the equivalents below each situation to help you. Answers at the back of the book.

1. Did you watch the debate on TV last night?

   Yes, it was quite a show. Who do you think was the winner?

   No question about it. The Conservatives _____ _____.

   I agree they probably had the better of it, but not by that much. I thought it was pretty close.

   won easily

   a gagné haut la main

   ganaron por mucho

   haben souverän (od. mühelos) gewonnen

   hanno vinto senza colpo ferire

I GUESS I GOT OFF ON THE WRONG FOOT.

2. Ted   Who do you think will get the Assistant Director General's position?

Roger   They say Roberts, Tremblay, Anderson and McKay (1) _____.

Alice   Well, I'd say you can cross Roberts off the list. He (2) _____.

Ted   What makes you say that?

Alice   Because from the day he joined he hasn't got on with the Director General. Poor guy. He just (3) _____ _____ and you know how important first impressions are to the D.G.

Roger   Mm, I know what you mean.

Ted   And I've heard through the grapevine that McKay's out of the running.

Alice   So it looks like Anderson or Tremblay.

Ted   Yes, they're pretty evenly matched. Either one of them would make a good A.D.G. I'd say (4) _____ _____ between Anderson and Tremblay.

Alice   I'd put my money on Anderson. She's really got what it takes. I think it's (5) _____ _____ for her.

Roger   Don't underestimate Tremblay. He is really sharp and very competent. He'd be my choice.

(1) are being considered as candidates

(2) has no chance of winning

(3) began badly

(4) their chances are equal

(5) certain

(1) sont en lice

(2) n'a aucune chance

(3) est parti du mauvais pied

(4) leurs chances sont égales

(5) l'affaire est dans le sac

(1) están en la lista

(2) no tiene posibilidad ninguna

(3) empezó mal; comenzó mal

(4) hay un empate

(5) de seguro

(1) liegen im Rennen

(2) hat keinerlei Chance

(3) hatte einen schlechten Start

(4) es ist völlig offen

(5) sie hat es in der Tasche

(1) sono in lizza

(2) no ha alcuna possibilità

(3) partito con il piede sbagliato

(4) lotta ad armi pari

(5) penso che ha la vittoria in tasca

3. Hey, did you hear? Maureen Marchand's been appointed head of marketing.

   Well, well! Sam isn't going to like that.

   You can say that again. He's been acting head for so long that he isn't going to like having to _____ to somebody else.

   No, he's never enjoyed playing second fiddle — and especially not to a woman.

be subordinate to

être le second violon

sich zurückhalten;
(die zweite Geige spielen)

ceder el lugar a

essere secondo a qualcuno

4. I'm afraid we've probably lost the Melson contract. They're not happy with the last series of commercials we did for them.

So I hear. But it's not lost yet. I've sent Andrew to try and talk them into giving us another chance.

Well, if anybody can persuade them, it's him.

Well, I think he might be able _____.

to succeed in the face of difficulties

réussir son coup   *lograrlo*

zuwege bringen   *fare il colpo*

5. You won't (1) _____ Jack.
He knows what he's talking about when it comes to marketing.

Usually, yes. But this time he really is (2) _____
_____. He wants to drop all the television advertising.
That's crazy. Nobody agrees with him.

If Jack says it's a good idea, he's probably right.

(1) win an argument against

(2) in an isolated position, with no one else agreeing

(1) le convaincre   *(1) podrás oponerte*

(2) completement seul, isolé   *(2) en una posición solitarià*

(1) du hast keinen Strich gegen   *(1) avere la meglio su*

(2) er steht ganz verlassen da   *(2) tagliato fuori*

TEST 3 (Chapters 11~15)

This is a test of some of the idioms in chapters 11-15.
An English equivalent is given for each item. The exact number of words required is indicated each time by the number of blanks. Use this test to check what you know either before or after you have studied Chapters 11-15. The answers are on page 96.

1. Come on. Get to the point. _____ _____ _____ _____

_____. I want a straight answer to my question.

don't avoid the question

2. Your argument is irrelevant. It's completely _____ _____

_____.

not on the subject

3. Has a final decision been made on the proposed move yet?
No, they haven't decided. It's still _____ _____ _____ _____.

undecided

4. I'd say Linda _____ _____ _____.
Aw, come on! I agree she won but not by that much.

won easily

ARE IN THE RUNNING

5. We're near agreement but the _____ _____ is how many Saturdays we can ask people to work each month.

problem point

6. Sally was left _____ _____ _____ _____. In the end, she was the only one who voted for Peter.

isolated

7. Don't run away Jack Brown, I've _____ _____ _____ _____ _____ _____ _____.

Oh, Oh! What have I done wrong this time?

something to argue about with you

8. If that clerk gives me any more trouble I'm going to _____ _____ _____ _____ and complain to the Bank Manager.

go to a higher authority than the person concerned.

9. You know I'm very interested in this project, so please _____ _____ _____.

Don't worry. I'll call you every week to let you know how things are going.

give me any new information

I'M AFRAID YOUR ARGUMENT DOESN'T HOLD WATER.

BILL'S GETTING A RUNDOWN.

10. My question couldn't have been more direct. I _____ her _____ _____ if my transfer request was approved.

asked the direct question

11. I've never really got on with my supervisor. Right from the very first day I _____ _____ _____ _____ _____ _____ with him.

began badly

12. I tell you it's high time this whole system was changed.

Come on now. The system isn't so bad. _____ _____ _____ _____. You'll only cause trouble for everybody.

don't try to upset the system

13. Can you show me how this calculator works? I've been trying to get a subtotal but I just _____ _____ _____ _____ _____ _____.

don't know how to make it work

14. I _____ _____ _____ you suggesting that my department was responsible for the mistake.

resent

15. I'd say Tom and Helen have an equal chance of winning the chess tournament.

I agree _____ _____ _____ between those two.

their chances are equal

16. Just give me a rough estimate.

Well, _____ _____ _____ _____ _____ _____ I'd say it'll cost about sixty thousand.

I guess, from memory

17. He won't accept blame or responsibility for anything.

He always tries to _____ _____ _____.

put the blame or responsibility on others

18. The other candidates are much better qualified than Stan. He _____ _____ _____ _____.

has no chance of success

19. If he thinks I'm going to accept such poor quality work he's _____ _____ a nasty shock.

certain to get

20. I'd be grateful if you would _____ _____ _____ _____ _____ _____. I want to know as soon as possible.

listen to see if you can find some information

94

Answers

1. **Time Expressions**
   1.b, 2.g, 3.e, 4.h, 5.d, 6.f, 7.a, 8.c, 9.j, 10.i.

2. **Being Confused**
   1.b, 2.g, 3.c, 4.j, 5.a, 6.e, 7.d, 8.f, 9.i, 10.h.

3. **Knowing or Agreeing**
   1.g, 2.f, 3.a, 4.j, 5.h, 6.c, 7.d, 8.e, 9.b, 10.i.

4. **Failure**
   1.h, 2.a, 3.g, 4.b, 5.c, 6.i, 7.j, 8.e, 9.d, 10.f.

5. **Success or Strong Interest**
   1.i, 2.d, 3.h, 4.j, 5.g, 6.c, 7.b, 8.a, 9.e, 10.f.

Test 1
   1. Beats me. 2. High time. 3. Rings a bell. 4. Turns me on. 5. Went like a bomb. 6. Getting out of hand. 7. Bit off more than I could chew. 8. On the blink. 9. Kill two birds with one stone. 10. Couldn't get a word in edgeways. 11. Was a flop. 12. Slipped my mind. 13. Once in a blue moon. 14. In the long run. 15. On the grapevine. 16. Straight from the horse's mouth. 17. Can't make head nor tail of. 18. Haven't got a leg to stand on. 19. Over the moon. 20. Knows the ropes.

6. **Money Matters**
   1.c, 2.b, 3.f, 4.d, 5.h, 6.g, 7.e, 8.a, 9.i, 10.j.

7. **Extremes or Excess**
   1.(1)a, (2)f, 2.d, 3.j, 4.b, 5.e, 6.i, 7.h, 8(1)g, (2)c.

8. **Compromise or Balance**
   1.f, 2.d, 3.c, 4.b, 5.a, 6.h, 7.e, 8.j, 9.g, 10.i.

9. **Complaining or Commiserating**
   1.e, 2.(1)d, (2)a, 3.f, 4.c, 5.(1)j, (2)g, 6.i, 7.h, 8.b.

10. Meeting People

1.a, 2.j, 3.f, 4.b, 5.d, 6.c, 7.(1)i, (2)h, 8.(1)e, (2)g.

Test 2.

1. Can't make ends meet. 2. Making a mountain out of a molehill.
3. Take . . . with a pinch of salt. 4. Was the last straw. 5. Talking shop.
6. Pulling his weight. 7. Selling like hot cakes. 8. Pay lip service to.
9. What a rip-off. 10. (1) Fed up to the teeth with. (2) Sits on the fence.
11. Bend over backwards. 12. (1) Bumping into. (2) It's a small world,
isn't it. 13. Pull the wool over other people's eyes. 14. Cut corners.
15. Splitting hairs. 16. Put my foot in it. 17. A happy medium. 18. Fob
me off.

11. Giving or Seeking Information

1.e, 2.d, 3.j, 4.a, 5.b, 6.i, 7.(1)f, (2)c, 8.h, 9.g.

12. Things Going Wrong

1.g, 2.e, 3.d, 4.(1)c, (2)a, 5.h, 6.i, 7.j, 8.f, 9.b.

13. Contradicting or Disagreeing

1.i, 2.c, 3.(1)g, (2)a, (3)e, (4)f, 4.b, 5.h, 6.j, 7.d.

14. The Bureaucracy

1.d, 2.g, 3.f, 4.b, 5.(1)i, (2)a, 6.c, 7.(1)h, (2)e, 8.j.

15. Winning or Losing

1.i, 2(1)a, (2)g, (3)c, (4)j, (5)d, 3e, 4.f, 5(1)b, (2)h.

Test 3.

1. Don't beat about the bush. 2. Beside the point. 3. Up in the air. 4.
Won hands down. 5. Stumbling block. 6. Out on a limb. 7. Got a bone
to pick with you. 8. Go over (his) head. 9. Keep me posted. 10. Asked
her point blank. 11. Got off on the wrong foot. 12. Don't rock the boat.
13. Can't get the hang of it. 14. Take exception to. 15. It's a toss-up. 16.
Off the top of my head. 17. Pass the buck. 18. Doesn't stand a chance. 19.
In for. 20. Keep your ear to the ground.